The Fcuking Gratitude Journal

This journal was designed based on my personal experience.

I am sure you go daily trhogh the same things:

People that drives you crazy

People that you really want give them a nice kick on their balls

things that I am glad I did

Things I am glad I did NOT do it

Also, I am sure you take you time to be thankfull for what

you have . There is space for it too!

I have been using this journal for quite some time for tracking things

and some stress relief.

have decided to share with you.

I hope you enjoy it as much as I do!

Date

Today was a great day because

Proud because I did...

Glad because I didn't

I am blessed because:

Who I wanted to kick on the balls today

Fucking things to do today:

_____
_____
_____
_____
_____
_____
_____
_____
_____

Shit someone else shoud have done it and now I have to fucking do it:

_____
_____
_____
_____
_____
_____
_____
_____

Date

Today was a great day because

Proud because I did...

Glad because I didn't

I am blessed because:

Who I wanted to kick on the balls today

Fucking things to do today:

_____

_____

_____

_____

_____

_____

_____

_____

Shit someone else shoud have done it and now I have to fucking do it:

_____

_____

_____

_____

_____

_____

_____

Date

Today was a great day because

Proud because I did...

Glad because I didn't

I am blessed because:

Who I wanted to kick on the balls today

Fucking things to do today:

_____
_____
_____
_____
_____
_____
_____
_____
_____

Shit someone else shoud have done it and now I have to fucking do it:

_____
_____
_____
_____
_____
_____
_____
_____

Date

Today was a great day because

Proud because I did...

Glad because I didn't

I am blessed because:

Who I wanted to kick on the balls today

Fucking things to do today:

_____
_____
_____
_____
_____
_____
_____
_____
_____

Shit someone else shoud have done it and now I have to fucking do it:

_____
_____
_____
_____
_____
_____
_____

Date

Today was a great day because

Proud because I did...

Glad because I didn't

I am blessed because:

Who I wanted to kick on the balls today

Fucking things to do today:

_____

_____

_____

_____

_____

_____

_____

_____

_____

Shit someone else shoud have done it and now I have to fucking do it:

_____

_____

_____

_____

_____

_____

_____

_____

Date

Today was a great day because

Proud because I did...

Glad because I didn't

I am blessed because:

Who I wanted to kick on the balls today

Fucking things to do today:

_____
_____
_____
_____
_____
_____
_____
_____

Shit someone else shoud have done it and now I have to fucking do it:

_____
_____
_____
_____
_____
_____
_____

Date

Today was a great day because

Proud because I did...

Glad because I didn't

I am blessed because:

Who I wanted to kick on the balls today

Fucking things to do today:

_____
_____
_____
_____
_____
_____
_____
_____
_____

Shit someone else shoud have done it and now I have to fucking do it:

_____
_____
_____
_____
_____
_____
_____

Date

Today was a great day because

Proud because I did...

Glad because I didn't

I am blessed because:

Who I wanted to kick on the balls today

Fucking things to do today:

_____

_____

_____

_____

_____

_____

_____

_____

Shit someone else shoud have done it and now I have to fucking do it:

_____

_____

_____

_____

_____

_____

_____

Date

Today was a great day because

Proud because I did...

Glad because I didn't

I am blessed because:

Who I wanted to kick on the balls today

Fucking things to do today:

_____
_____
_____
_____
_____
_____
_____
_____
_____

Shit someone else shoud have done it and now I have to fucking do it:

_____
_____
_____
_____
_____
_____
_____

Date

Today was a great day because

Proud because I did...

Glad because I didn't

I am blessed because:

Who I wanted to kick on the balls today

Fucking things to do today:

_____

_____

_____

_____

_____

_____

_____

_____

Shit someone else shoud have done it and now I have to fucking do it:

_____

_____

_____

_____

_____

_____

_____

_____

Date

Today was a great day because

Proud because I did...

Glad because I didn't

I am blessed because:

Who I wanted to kick on the balls today

Fucking things to do today:

_____

_____

_____

_____

_____

_____

_____

_____

Shit someone else shoud have done it and now I have to fucking do it:

_____

_____

_____

_____

_____

_____

_____

Date

Today was a great day because

Proud because I did...

Glad because I didn't

I am blessed because:

Who I wanted to kick on the balls today

Fucking things to do today:

_____

_____

_____

_____

_____

_____

_____

_____

Shit someone else shoud have done it and now I have to fucking do it:

_____

_____

_____

_____

_____

_____

_____

Date

Today was a great day because

Proud because I did...

Glad because I didn't

I am blessed because:

Who I wanted to kick on the balls today

Fucking things to do today:

_____
_____
_____
_____
_____
_____
_____
_____
_____

Shit someone else shoud have done it and now I have to fucking do it:

_____
_____
_____
_____
_____
_____
_____

Date

Today was a great day because

Proud because I did...

Glad because I didn't

I am blessed because:

Who I wanted to kick on the balls today

Fucking things to do today:

_____

_____

_____

_____

_____

_____

_____

_____

Shit someone else shoud have done it and now I have to fucking do it:

_____

_____

_____

_____

_____

_____

Date

Today was a great day because

Proud because I did...

Glad because I didn't

I am blessed because:

Who I wanted to kick on the balls today

Fucking things to do today:

_____

_____

_____

_____

_____

_____

_____

_____

_____

Shit someone else shoud have done it and now I have to fucking do it:

_____

_____

_____

_____

_____

_____

_____

_____

Date

Today was a great day because

Proud because I did...

Glad because I didn't

I am blessed because:

Who I wanted to kick on the balls today

Fucking things to do today:

_____
_____
_____
_____
_____
_____
_____
_____

Shit someone else shoud have done it and now I have to fucking do it:

_____
_____
_____
_____
_____
_____

Date

Today was a great day because

Proud because I did...

Glad because I didn't

I am blessed because:

Who I wanted to kick on the balls today

Fucking things to do today:

_____
_____
_____
_____
_____
_____
_____
_____
_____

Shit someone else shoud have done it and now I have to fucking do it:

_____
_____
_____
_____
_____
_____
_____

Date

Today was a great day because

Proud because I did...

Glad because I didn't

I am blessed because:

Who I wanted to kick on the balls today

Fucking things to do today:

_____

_____

_____

_____

_____

_____

_____

_____

Shit someone else shoud have done it and now I have to fucking do it:

_____

_____

_____

_____

_____

_____

_____

Date

Today was a great day because

Proud because I did...

Glad because I didn't

I am blessed because:

Who I wanted to kick on the balls today

Fucking things to do today:

_____
_____
_____
_____
_____
_____
_____
_____
_____
_____

Shit someone else shoud have done it and now I have to fucking do it:

_____
_____
_____
_____
_____
_____
_____
_____

Date

Today was a great day because

Proud because I did...

Glad because I didn't

I am blessed because:

Who I wanted to kick on the balls today

Fucking things to do today:

_____
_____
_____
_____
_____
_____
_____
_____
_____
_____

Shit someone else shoud have done it and now I have to fucking do it:

_____
_____
_____
_____
_____
_____
_____
_____
_____

Date

Today was a great day because

Proud because I did...

Glad because I didn't

I am blessed because:

Who I wanted to kick on the balls today

Fucking things to do today:

_____

_____

_____

_____

_____

_____

_____

_____

Shit someone else shoud have done it and now I have to fucking do it:

_____

_____

_____

_____

_____

_____

_____

_____

Date

Today was a great day because

Proud because I did...

Glad because I didn't

I am blessed because:

Who I wanted to kick on the balls today

Fucking things to do today:

_____

_____

_____

_____

_____

_____

_____

_____

Shit someone else shoud have done it and now I have to fucking do it:

_____

_____

_____

_____

_____

_____

Date

Today was a great day because

Proud because I did...

Glad because I didn't

I am blessed because:

Who I wanted to kick on the balls today

Fucking things to do today:

_____

_____

_____

_____

_____

_____

_____

_____

Shit someone else shoud have done it and now I have to fucking do it:

_____

_____

_____

_____

_____

_____

_____

Date

Today was a great day because

Proud because I did...

Glad because I didn't

I am blessed because:

Who I wanted to kick on the balls today

Fucking things to do today:

_____
_____
_____
_____
_____
_____
_____
_____
_____

Shit someone else shoud have done it and now I have to fucking do it:

_____
_____
_____
_____
_____
_____
_____
_____

Date

Today was a great day because

Proud because I did...

Glad because I didn't

I am blessed because:

Who I wanted to kick on the balls today

Fucking things to do today:

_____
_____
_____
_____
_____
_____
_____
_____

Shit someone else shoud have done it and now I have to fucking do it:

_____
_____
_____
_____
_____
_____
_____

Date

Today was a great day because

Proud because I did...

Glad because I didn't

I am blessed because:

Who I wanted to kick on the balls today

Fucking things to do today:

_____

_____

_____

_____

_____

_____

_____

_____

Shit someone else shoud have done it and now I have to fucking do it:

_____

_____

_____

_____

_____

_____

_____

_____

Date

Today was a great day because

Proud because I did...

Glad because I didn't

I am blessed because:

Who I wanted to kick on the balls today

Fucking things to do today:

_____
_____
_____
_____
_____
_____
_____
_____
_____

Shit someone else shoud have done it and now I have to fucking do it:

_____
_____
_____
_____
_____
_____
_____
_____

Date

Today was a great day because

Proud because I did...

Glad because I didn't

I am blessed because:

Who I wanted to kick on the balls today

Fucking things to do today:

_____

_____

_____

_____

_____

_____

_____

_____

Shit someone else shoud have done it and now I have to fucking do it:

_____

_____

_____

_____

_____

_____

_____

Date

Today was a great day because

Proud because I did...

Glad because I didn't

I am blessed because:

Who I wanted to kick on the balls today

Fucking things to do today:

_____

_____

_____

_____

_____

_____

_____

Shit someone else shoud have done it and now I have to fucking do it:

_____

_____

_____

_____

_____

_____

Date

Today was a great day because

Proud because I did...

Glad because I didn't

I am blessed because:

Who I wanted to kick on the balls today

Fucking things to do today:

_____
_____
_____
_____
_____
_____
_____
_____
_____

Shit someone else shoud have done it and now I have to fucking do it:

_____
_____
_____
_____
_____
_____
_____

Date

Today was a great day because

Proud because I did…

Glad because I didn't

I am blessed because:

Who I wanted to kick on the balls today

Fucking things to do today:

_____
_____
_____
_____
_____
_____
_____
_____
_____

Shit someone else shoud have done it and now I have to fucking do it:

_____
_____
_____
_____
_____
_____
_____

Date

Today was a great day because

Proud because I did...

Glad because I didn't

I am blessed because:

Who I wanted to kick on the balls today

Fucking things to do today:

_____
_____
_____
_____
_____
_____
_____
_____
_____

Shit someone else shoud have done it and now I have to fucking do it:

_____
_____
_____
_____
_____
_____
_____

Date

Today was a great day because

Proud because I did...

Glad because I didn't

I am blessed because:

Who I wanted to kick on the balls today

Fucking things to do today:

_____

_____

_____

_____

_____

_____

_____

_____

Shit someone else shoud have done it and now I have to fucking do it:

_____

_____

_____

_____

_____

_____

Date

Today was a great day because

Proud because I did...

Glad because I didn't

I am blessed because:

Who I wanted to kick on the balls today

Fucking things to do today:

_____
_____
_____
_____
_____
_____
_____
_____

Shit someone else shoud have done it and now I have to fucking do it:

_____
_____
_____
_____
_____
_____
_____
_____

Date

Today was a great day because

Proud because I did...

Glad because I didn't

I am blessed because:

Who I wanted to kick on the balls today

Fucking things to do today:

_____
_____
_____
_____
_____
_____
_____
_____

Shit someone else shoud have done it and now I have to fucking do it:

_____
_____
_____
_____
_____
_____
_____

Date

Today was a great day because

Proud because I did...

Glad because I didn't

I am blessed because:

Who I wanted to kick on the balls today

Fucking things to do today:

_____
_____
_____
_____
_____
_____
_____
_____
_____

Shit someone else shoud have done it and now I have to fucking do it:

_____
_____
_____
_____
_____
_____
_____
_____

Date

Today was a great day because

Proud because I did...

Glad because I didn't

I am blessed because:

Who I wanted to kick on the balls today

Fucking things to do today:

_____
_____
_____
_____
_____
_____
_____
_____
_____
_____

Shit someone else shoud have done it and now I have to fucking do it:

_____
_____
_____
_____
_____
_____
_____
_____

Date

Today was a great day because

Proud because I did...

Glad because I didn't

I am blessed because:

Who I wanted to kick on the balls today

Fucking things to do today:

_____
_____
_____
_____
_____
_____
_____
_____
_____

Shit someone else shoud have done it and now I have to fucking do it:

_____
_____
_____
_____
_____
_____
_____
_____

Date

Today was a great day because

Proud because I did...

Glad because I didn't

I am blessed because:

Who I wanted to kick on the balls today

Fucking things to do today:

_____

_____

_____

_____

_____

_____

_____

_____

Shit someone else shoud have done it and now I have to fucking do it:

_____

_____

_____

_____

_____

_____

Date

Today was a great day because

Proud because I did...

Glad because I didn't

I am blessed because:

Who I wanted to kick on the balls today

Fucking things to do today:

_____
_____
_____
_____
_____
_____
_____
_____

Shit someone else shoud have done it and now I have to fucking do it:

_____
_____
_____
_____
_____
_____

Date

Today was a great day because

Proud because I did...

Glad because I didn't

I am blessed because:

Who I wanted to kick on the balls today

Fucking things to do today:

_____
_____
_____
_____
_____
_____
_____
_____

Shit someone else shoud have done it and now I have to fucking do it:

_____
_____
_____
_____
_____
_____
_____

Date

Today was a great day because

Proud because I did...

Glad because I didn't

I am blessed because:

Who I wanted to kick on the balls today

Fucking things to do today:

_____
_____
_____
_____
_____
_____
_____
_____
_____

Shit someone else shoud have done it and now I have to fucking do it:

_____
_____
_____
_____
_____
_____
_____
_____

Date

Today was a great day because

Proud because I did...

Glad because I didn't

I am blessed because:

Who I wanted to kick on the balls today

Fucking things to do today:

_____

_____

_____

_____

_____

_____

_____

_____

Shit someone else shoud have done it and now I have to fucking do it:

_____

_____

_____

_____

_____

_____

_____

Date

Today was a great day because

Proud because I did...

Glad because I didn't

I am blessed because:

Who I wanted to kick on the balls today

Fucking things to do today:

_____
_____
_____
_____
_____
_____
_____
_____
_____

Shit someone else shoud have done it and now I have to fucking do it:

_____
_____
_____
_____
_____
_____
_____
_____

Date

Today was a great day because

Proud because I did...

Glad because I didn't

I am blessed because:

Who I wanted to kick on the balls today

Fucking things to do today:

_____
_____
_____
_____
_____
_____
_____
_____
_____

Shit someone else shoud have done it and now I have to fucking do it:

_____
_____
_____
_____
_____
_____
_____
_____

Date

Today was a great day because

Proud because I did...

Glad because I didn't

I am blessed because:

Who I wanted to kick on the balls today

Fucking things to do today:

_____

_____

_____

_____

_____

_____

_____

_____

Shit someone else shoud have done it and now I have to fucking do it:

_____

_____

_____

_____

_____

_____

_____

Date

Today was a great day because

Proud because I did...

Glad because I didn't

I am blessed because:

Who I wanted to kick on the balls today

Fucking things to do today:

_____

_____

_____

_____

_____

_____

_____

_____

Shit someone else shoud have done it and now I have to fucking do it:

_____

_____

_____

_____

_____

_____

_____

Date

Today was a great day because

Proud because I did...

Glad because I didn't

I am blessed because:

Who I wanted to kick on the balls today

Fucking things to do today:

_____

_____

_____

_____

_____

_____

_____

_____

Shit someone else shoud have done it and now I have to fucking do it:

_____

_____

_____

_____

_____

_____

_____

Date

Today was a great day because

Proud because I did...

Glad because I didn't

I am blessed because:

Who I wanted to kick on the balls today

Fucking things to do today:

_____

_____

_____

_____

_____

_____

_____

_____

Shit someone else shoud have done it and now I have to fucking do it:

_____

_____

_____

_____

_____

_____

Date

Today was a great day because

Proud because I did...

Glad because I didn't

I am blessed because:

Who I wanted to kick on the balls today

Fucking things to do today:

_____
_____
_____
_____
_____
_____
_____
_____

Shit someone else shoud have done it and now I have to fucking do it:

_____
_____
_____
_____
_____
_____
_____

Date

Today was a great day because

Proud because I did...

Glad because I didn't

I am blessed because:

Who I wanted to kick on the balls today

Fucking things to do today:

_____

_____

_____

_____

_____

_____

_____

_____

Shit someone else shoud have done it and now I have to fucking do it:

_____

_____

_____

_____

_____

_____

_____

_____

Date

Today was a great day because

Proud because I did...

Glad because I didn't

I am blessed because:

Who I wanted to kick on the balls today

Fucking things to do today:

_____
_____
_____
_____
_____
_____
_____
_____
_____

Shit someone else shoud have done it and now I have to fucking do it:

_____
_____
_____
_____
_____
_____
_____
_____

Date

Today was a great day because

Proud because I did...

Glad because I didn't

I am blessed because:

Who I wanted to kick on the balls today

Fucking things to do today:

_____

_____

_____

_____

_____

_____

_____

_____

Shit someone else shoud have done it and now I have to fucking do it:

_____

_____

_____

_____

_____

_____

_____

Date

Today was a great day because

Proud because I did...

Glad because I didn't

I am blessed because:

Who I wanted to kick on the balls today

Fucking things to do today:

_____
_____
_____
_____
_____
_____
_____
_____
_____

Shit someone else shoud have done it and now I have to fucking do it:

_____
_____
_____
_____
_____
_____
_____
_____

Date

Today was a great day because

Proud because I did...

Glad because I didn't

I am blessed because:

Who I wanted to kick on the balls today

Fucking things to do today:

_____
_____
_____
_____
_____
_____
_____
_____

Shit someone else shoud have done it and now I have to fucking do it:

_____
_____
_____
_____
_____
_____

Date

Today was a great day because

Proud because I did...

Glad because I didn't

I am blessed because:

Who I wanted to kick on the balls today

Fucking things to do today:

_____
_____
_____
_____
_____
_____
_____
_____
_____

Shit someone else shoud have done it and now I have to fucking do it:

_____
_____
_____
_____
_____
_____
_____
_____

Date

Today was a great day because

Proud because I did...

Glad because I didn't

I am blessed because:

Who I wanted to kick on the balls today

Fucking things to do today:

_____
_____
_____
_____
_____
_____
_____

Shit someone else shoud have done it and now I have to fucking do it:

_____
_____
_____
_____
_____
_____
_____

Date

Today was a great day because

Proud because I did...

Glad because I didn't

I am blessed because:

Who I wanted to kick on the balls today

Fucking things to do today:

_____
_____
_____
_____
_____
_____
_____
_____

Shit someone else shoud have done it and now I have to fucking do it:

_____
_____
_____
_____
_____
_____
_____

Date

Today was a great day because

Proud because I did...

Glad because I didn't

I am blessed because:

Who I wanted to kick on the balls today

Fucking things to do today:

_____
_____
_____
_____
_____
_____
_____
_____

Shit someone else shoud have done it and now I have to fucking do it:

_____
_____
_____
_____
_____
_____
_____

Date

Today was a great day because

Proud because I did...

Glad because I didn't

I am blessed because:

Who I wanted to kick on the balls today

Fucking things to do today:

_____
_____
_____
_____
_____
_____
_____
_____

Shit someone else shoud have done it and now I have to fucking do it:

_____
_____
_____
_____
_____
_____
_____